# U.S. NATIONAL PARKS
# YOSEMITE NATIONAL PARK

by Penelope S. Nelson

pogo

# Ideas for Parents and Teachers

Pogo Books let children practice reading informational text while introducing them to nonfiction features such as headings, labels, sidebars, maps, and diagrams, as well as a table of contents, glossary, and index.

Carefully leveled text with a strong photo match offers early fluent readers the support they need to succeed.

## Before Reading

- "Walk" through the book and point out the various nonfiction features. Ask the student what purpose each feature serves.
- Look at the glossary together. Read and discuss the words.

## Read the Book

- Have the child read the book independently.
- Invite him or her to list questions that arise from reading.

## After Reading

- Discuss the child's questions. Talk about how he or she might find answers to those questions.
- Prompt the child to think more. Ask: Yosemite National Park was made a national park because of its special landscape. Can you think of another place that should be a national park? Why?

Pogo Books are published by Jump!
5357 Penn Avenue South
Minneapolis, MN 55419
www.jumplibrary.com

Library of Congress Cataloging-in-Publication Data

Names: Nelson, Penelope, 1994- author.
Title: Yosemite National Park / by Penelope S. Nelson.
Description: Pogo books edition.
Minneapolis, MN: Jump!, [2020]
Series: U.S. National Parks | Includes index.
Audience: Ages 7-10.
Identifiers: LCCN 2018056011 (print)
LCCN 2018056257 (ebook)
ISBN 9781641288187 (ebook)
ISBN 9781641288170 (hardcover : alk. paper)
Subjects: LCSH: Yosemite National Park (Calif.)
Juvenile literature.
Classification: LCC F868.Y6 (ebook)
LCC F868.Y6 N47 2020 (print)
DDC 979.4/47—dc23
LC record available at https://lccn.loc.gov/2018056011

Editor: Jenna Trnka
Designer: Jenna Casura

Photo Credits: tonda/iStock, cover, 4; canadastock/Shutterstock, 1; Eloi_Omella/iStock, 3; Robert Bohrer/Shutterstock, 5, 23; rmbarricarte/iStock, 6-7; windsketch/Shutterstock, 8-9; Martina Bimbaum/Shutterstock, 10; uschools/iStock, 11; Gregory B Cuvelier/Shutterstock, 12-13; Pavliha/iStock, 14-15; Dudarev Mikhail/Shutterstock, 16-17; Duncan Selby/Alamy, 18; Paula Solloway/Alamy, 19; Aflo Co., Ltd/Alamy, 20-21.

Printed in the United States of America at Corporate Graphics in North Mankato, Minnesota.

# TABLE OF CONTENTS

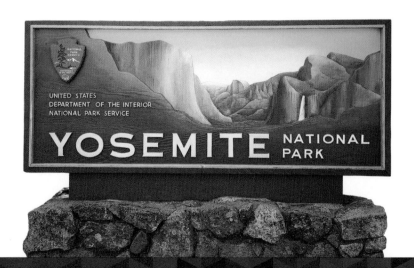

# CHAPTER 1

# FORMED BY GLACIERS

Do you like to hike? Would you like to see one of the tallest waterfalls in the United States? Yosemite Falls is 2,425 feet (739 meters) tall!

Yosemite Falls

Let's explore Yosemite National Park! This national park is in California. The U.S. government runs it. Why? It protects the land, animals, and plants. Around 1,450 **species** of wildflowers can be found here!

Wander through **groves** of giant sequoias. These trees can grow to be around 300 feet (91 m) tall! They can live for more than 3,000 years!

See the Grizzly Giant in Mariposa Grove. It is the park's most famous tree. Scientists think it is around 1,800 years old!

## WHAT DO YOU THINK?

Many animals live here. See bears, bats, and mountain lions. About 260 species of birds are in the park.
Why do you think so many animals live here?
What animals live near you?

Grizzly
Giant

Yosemite Valley

This park is in the Sierra Nevada mountain range. **Glaciers** formed the landscape. This was more than 10,000 years ago! They formed **peaks**, domes, and valleys. Yosemite Valley is in the heart of the park.

# TAKE A LOOK!

Glaciers here were first mapped in 1883. They have changed since. How? Warmer temperatures melt them. They are shrinking.

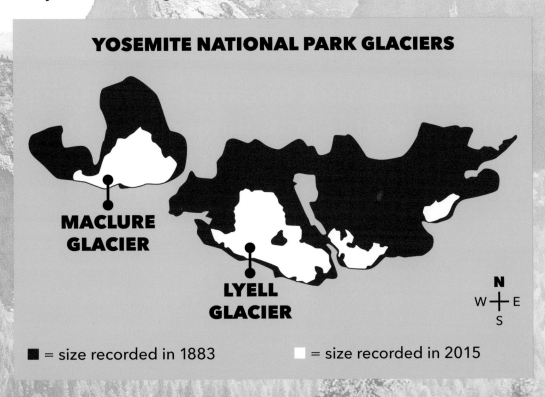

**YOSEMITE NATIONAL PARK GLACIERS**

MACLURE GLACIER

LYELL GLACIER

N
W — E
S

■ = size recorded in 1883     □ = size recorded in 2015

# CHAPTER 2

# EXPLORE THE PARK

The incredible rock formations of Yosemite Valley make this park unique. Half Dome is a large **granite** dome. It rises almost 5,000 feet (1,524 m) above the valley floor.

**Half Dome**

El Capitan rises nearly straight up! It is more than 3,000 feet (914 m) tall. Experienced rock climbers love this wall of granite. Merced River is at its base.

El Capitan

Merced River

Horsetail
Fall . . . . . . ▶

Many waterfalls fall over
these rocks. Yosemite Falls
is one. Horsetail Fall is another.
In the month of February,
it looks like it is on fire.
Why? The water reflects
the sunset. Pretty!

**DID YOU KNOW?**

You can see rainbows at
night in the park! The full
moon gives light to see
**moonbows** at many of
the waterfalls in the park.

Mount Hoffmann is in the center of the park. Hike to the top for great views. Hike to Tenaya Lake for a swim. Or kayak in the lake!

Tenaya Lake

Do you like to camp? The park has
13 campgrounds to choose from.
Those in Yosemite Valley are busier.
**Backcountry** sites are quieter.
But be ready to hike there!
You can also stay in a lodge
or hotel in the park.

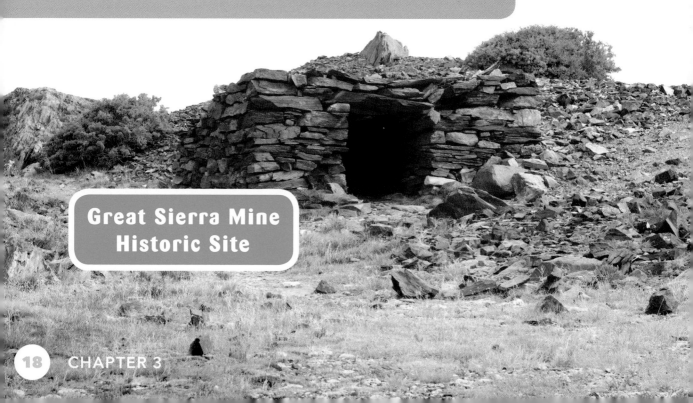

# CHAPTER 3

## PEOPLE IN THE PARK

People have lived in this area for many years. Native Americans were the first. White **settlers** came here to **mine**. You can still see some of the old mines!

Great Sierra Mine
Historic Site

Artists helped make this area a national park. They painted and took pictures of the valley. People still make art here today!

Glacier Point

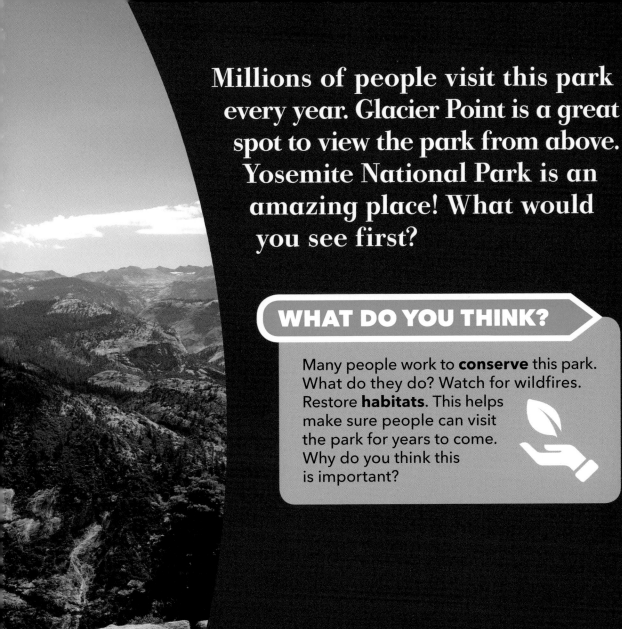

Millions of people visit this park every year. Glacier Point is a great spot to view the park from above. Yosemite National Park is an amazing place! What would you see first?

## WHAT DO YOU THINK?

Many people work to **conserve** this park. What do they do? Watch for wildfires. Restore **habitats**. This helps make sure people can visit the park for years to come. Why do you think this is important?

# QUICK FACTS & TOOLS

CALIFORNIA

Sierra Nevada mountain range

Tenaya Lake

• Great Sierra Mine

Yosemite Falls •
• Half Dome
• Glacier Point
Yosemite Valley

• Mariposa Grove

■ = Yosemite National Park

N
W — E
S

## YOSEMITE NATIONAL PARK

**Location:** California

**Year Established:** 1890

**Area:** 761,266 acres (308,073 hectares)

**Approximate Yearly Visitors:** 4 million

**Top Attractions:**
Glacier Point, Mariposa Grove, Yosemite Falls

**Total Length of Hiking Trails:**
800 miles (1,287 kilometers)

## GLOSSARY

**backcountry:** Underdeveloped, rural areas.

**conserve:** To protect something, such as animals, plants, and land, from loss.

**glaciers:** Large, slow-moving masses of ice.

**granite:** Hard, gray rock.

**groves:** Small groups of trees with little or no underbrush.

**habitats:** The places where certain animals and plants are usually found.

**mine:** To dig up minerals that are in the ground.

**moonbows:** Rainbows formed by moonlight.

**peaks:** The pointed tops of high mountains.

**settlers:** People who move to a new region or colony to live.

**species:** One of the groups into which similar animals and plants are divided.

# INDEX

# TO LEARN MORE

**Finding more information is as easy as 1, 2, 3.**

① **Go to www.factsurfer.com**

② **Enter "YosemiteNationalPark" into the search box.**

③ **Choose your book to see a list of websites.**

**FACT SURFER**